The Sky Is Great

the Sky Is Blue

Sharon Chmielarz

ISBN 978-0-9829335-0-3

Cover art
"In the Shadow of Morning Light," oil on canvas by Clinton Rost.
www.clintonrost.com
Used by permission of the artist.

Back cover photo by Norbert Marklin

Book and cover design by Joel Van Valin

Printed in the United States of America

WHISTLING SHADE
PRESS
www.whistlingshade.com

"...maybe, it would puzzle us
To find our way Home—"
- Emily Dickinson
  #224

Acknowledgments

These poems, or a version of them, were first published in the following magazines:

"Guards in the Pushkin Museum," "He Leadeth Me Beside the Still Waters," "An Evening of Klezmer," "Bells," "Telegram," "Sparse Music," "The Gus I Knew" - *Whistling Shade*

"Garden Scene" - *What Light*

"The Animals" - *Notre Dame Review*

"Cow, a Pastoral," "Headstones" - *County Lines, an Anthology*

"Lilacs" - *Ascent*

"The Kiss" - *Speakeasy*

"Everything," "Praise to Gourds" - *Dust & Fire*

"Goosegirl" - *Tin Coyote*

"Last Syllables" - *Louisiana Literature*

"Reins," "Pattern" - *Loonfeather*

"Zippers" - *Poetry East*

"The Accent on Flat" - *Sidewalks*

"For the Woman Who Gave Her Last Coin" - *Rag Mag*

"Tomatoes," "Table" - *Main Channel Voices*

"The Story of Diana and Actaeon" - *Ekphrasis*

"Six Days After" - *Minneapolis Quarterly Review*

"New Water" - *American Life in Poetry*

"Along the Wall, Jakuba ul" - *Kritya, a Journal of Poetry*

"An Evening of Klezmer" was also published in *Nowa Okolica Poetów*, trans. Janusz Zalewski.

"Reins" was also published in *beloved on the earth*, Holy Cow! Press.

"New Water" was also published in *The Millennium Reader*, 5th Edition, Prentice Hall.

"Chopin: Apples" was published in *Chopin with Cherries*, Moonrise Press.

"Zippers" was also published in *Poetry East's* anthology, *Seasons*.

"Tomatoes" and "The Story of Diana and Actaeon" were nominated for a Pushcart Prize.

Special thanks to Britt Fleming: Ten of these poems began as responses to stimuli shown on Northography.com.

Grateful acknowledgment is made to Whistling Shade Press and its editor and publisher, Joel Van Valin, for his often unsung work.

To Readers, gratefully

Contents

Table   12

I

An Evening of Klezmer   14
Along the Wall, Jakuba ul   15
The Vistula   16
Off Rynek Glowny   17
Garden Scene   18
Chopin: Apples   19
Oświęcim (Auschwitz)   20
Pattern   21
Melancholy Hour   22
Bells   23

II

Storm   26
The Past Is   27
Bed   28
Tomatoes   29
Tree Shadow   30
How to Take This   31
A House   32
A Perspective: Lighthouse Reached by Dock   33
At Work   34
Another House   35
Recognition   36
Reins   37
Phenomenon   38

III

To Live	40
The Accent on Flat	41
He Leadeth Me Beside the Still Waters	42
On the Ocean's Beach	43
Birch Trees	44
Moon	45
Six Days After	46
Last Syllables	47
Sparse Music	48
Orpheus's Shadow	49
Gourds	50
Lilacs	51
Headstones	52
Navigation by Metaphor	53
Cow, a Pastoral	54
The Animals	55
In Ascent	56
New Water	57

IV

Life Is Such a Great Beast	60
The Kiss	61
Zippers	62
Guards in the Pushkin Museum	63
Telegram	64
For the Woman Who Gave Her Last Coin	65
Story of a Farm Girl	66
The Queen: On the Occasion of the King's Burial	67
Goosegirl	68
Bar Scene	70

The Gus I Knew   71
In Sickness and in Health   72
So Many Kinds of Theatre   73
The Widow's Door   74
The Story of Diana and Actaeon   75
Juggling   76
Everything   77

Table

The table is green. A green table.
It sat so long under the leaves
it turned jealous and green.
Then all the dishes wanted to green, too.
And every one that sat down.
We all turned green. Look!
Our mossy hands. In summer
everything wants to be green.
Only the flowers say no.
And the sky. The sky says, *I'm great.*
I'm up here alone. I'm blue.

.

I

An Evening of Klezmer

for Tad

Like a ghost town, the Jewish quarter,
where you can hear church bells.
We didn't like being outside, alone.
We put our faces up to paned
windows and peered in.
People sat inside, at small tables,
walled in by drink and music.
A clarinetist played, moving
as if something long hidden
was being found. We wanted to go
inside where people were laughing
and clapping, but there was no room.
We hung around and waited,
watching for an opening,
but no one inside wanted to get out.

Along the Wall, *Jakuba ul*

I met the old woman who lives in Kazimierz,
walking her small dog one evening.
She looked up long enough to throw me a glance.
How much you have, Foreigner, it said.
How is it you deserve two canes?
She wore a gray coat; the dog's was black.
The door they entered I'd call squalid,
the stairs they climbed looked to me like despair.

And yet the little dog's tail was wagging,
playing, as if a little higher, a little closer
to the sun, grey turned to silver, pallor
into rose and the greatest happiness
that could befall them now,
would be a centimeter of new snow.

The Vistula

She is long and lazy. It's her toenails I see
flashing in the sun. A shiny paint job;
people love how she is old and young.

It's the same all over the world. An eye
falls on a spot along a curvy river and fifteen
thousand years later it's a city or town,

ruined several times over by war.
Once in a while not.
I saw a blue tent camping sleepily

on the Vistula's banks.
And Kraków's bridges
come from a hundred years ago.

Off Rynek Glowny

a square in Kraków

About the young woman who works in the post office:
How lovely she sits in her cage. So lively, so helpful,
selling the prettiest of Polish stamps, swinging from her
    perch
to fill our order. Ah, yes, she has postcards, too.
She lays them on the counter like colored eggs.
Look, she sings, which do you want?
Pray she won't grow old and lumpy in her box.
Like the rheumy ones who peer from kiosk windows.
Even the light in their eyes has gone gray.

Garden Scene

painting by Stanislav Zhukovski, 1873-1944;
d. in Prushkov Concentration Camp near Warsaw

The garden's divided in half by a picket fence.
On the closer side, a small table,
clothed and adorned by the useful
cup and tea pot, saucer, spoon,
painted in times when it was possible

to go into the house and find
a plate of bread to carry out.
To sit, to eat, to drink
under an awning of birch leaves,
near a flowerbed wash of swamp-red pinks.

Such a plain scene to fall in love with,
I want to gaze and gaze. It keeps
the heart beating in times of scarcity,
a garden in dreams from across a sea,
where one becomes full merely by remembering.

Chopin: Apples

And what country hasn't he lived in,
his music chilling the listener's arms?

And when haven't his glissandos
spilled over history, the colossus

that upsets lives like apple carts?
Apples rolling over cobbles.

God-fall we think,
finding among the bruised,

a handful of sweet apples.
The easy thank you is listening

to someone playing at a window
in Warsaw, turning the rumble

of despair into a mazurka.
"Beloved little corpse," Sand called Chopin,

sitting beside him at the keyboard.
Her "angel." His music, his wings.

Oświęcim (Auschwitz)

We didn't take the A4 out of Kraków.
We drove to Oświęcim on back roads,
a good chance to see the countryside,
village houses, prettily painted. Cats
in windows, dahlias and hollyhocks
bursting in gardens, a farmer woman
whose skirt hem trailed over cabbages
as she chopped off a head with a hand scythe.

My friend Bettijane says if she had a daughter
she wouldn't let her visit Auschwitz.
My friend Barb says her daughter got scared
just reading *Number the Stars*. But who
would be frightened in this village now?
I watched a woman with a brown shopping bag
get out of a city bus, walk past the house
where the German *Kommandant* once lived
with his family and pets. She slipped out
of sight through his ordinary garden gate.

Pattern

Alone at the window, narrow glass doors open.
From a manor's grounds an old breeze spills in.
Lace curtains flow around the round table and lamp,
Maybe twenty, thirty, forty years old. I feel
Under the shade's fringed hem for the switch;
An amber stage appears on the table's cloth,
An audience of shadows, hints and intonations,
A vague sense of recollection, a touch of warmth,
A chance for anyone from the past to appear,
To walk into this dusk; alive, happy, talking.

Melancholy Hour

Evening. A robin completes its roster of spring calls,
like the trumpeter of Kraków, ending the day,
calling its facts, recalling even the bleakest

happiness in small trills of delight.
Day, I retire, he sings. *Now I retire for the day.*

I, in my house, listen, admiring how well
he's made his house, so it brings great joy
when he returns to it, singing.

Not a small observation, Master Robin.
You've built your nest much better than I.

Bells

Never whining after holing
themselves up in a room for hours,

tolling
to the full
ends of their leashes,

not dwelling on their sounds'
sure demise.

Easily understandable.
Is as in 'just is.' So,

is.
Is as is.
Is.

Ringing,
clanging,

> over the park,
> across the gray, hobbled sky,

hoarse with *amour,*
trained to call,
"Home. Home."

II

Storm

You were the chosen, blessed
by the only real lesson. Once
you might have rent your clothes,
strewn ash in your hair. Even

a stranger upon seeing you,
would know you'd not been spared.
Not that your life was perfect before,
but intact: you were loved

and rich and strong, reduced now
to sifting through splinters,
your hands full of the invisible,
remnants, how an hour used to go.

The hard day comes, the day
of dry eyes. You must exit the rubble,
defeated. Of the great two-story house,
you pocket a single thimble.

The Past Is

I thought I was done with that
nightmare-ish mess, an old

and gnarly atlas of mistakes,
the wooden image of ache,

the ultimate stumbling
block, at best kept

in its over-crowded world,
underground, undercover,

under here, where I thought
I'd hidden it yesterday.

Bed

You've provided for the idyllic;
I have messed it up.

Yours, the proper stage for the night;
mine, the panzer dreams.

Your duty is stout, four-legged.
My visits, blindly neglectful.

Yours, the reality of pillow, mattress.
Mine, the illusions.

Some slight goodness within me
gives you thanks.

Tomatoes

Today I have eaten a perfect tomato.
A taste as singular as a voice, a full-
throated Russian soprano's, breathing
the end of summer and sunlight itself.
Nothing as social as in Mr. Neruda's ode.

Can I help it if I gorge on a second?
(In secret.) Or heighten, like a glutton,
the flavor of juicy pulp with salt?
Red, what I crave during winter, why
I dream of zinnias, their lack of discipline.

My Eden's apple, I eat you over the sink.
Childhood, granted a bit more sugar,
loneliness, plumped by sun and water.
Brilliant and common as the moon.
But much fleshier, much more human.

Tree Shadow

Late fall. The branches' shadows
limn house walls, windows,
sheer curtains, these, ordered

from a catalog where you read
the price, not the words.
According to cost, the least.

She browsed the entire stock,
sighed over those she liked best,
but chose these, patternless.

For the eye loves the beautiful
martyrdom of sheer barrenness,
fallen from a dream's caution.

How to Take This

It's hard to believe I live in anything
       a lovely kettle of take
so beautiful. Where an orchard bloomed,
       take it as home
I could plant lilacs. The view
       taking it in
glimmers in moonlight and sunlight, a blue
       taking hold of
a stream. Breathtaking, the light in grass,
       the take, the take of,
spring light's the gentlest, before it's worn
and low. Is it all in the mind?
       Take it anyway.

A House

This is a make-do place,
a house like the old rugged cross,
a house some woman wanted
to get out of, a house she had
one nice window to stand behind,
another installed later when it was
obvious she was stuck there,
in danger of the next strong gust,
in rooms someone left
behind and someone else found;
a house rented out each summer
to some poor, slucker writer,
a house a painter found
and did and made a million.
An old carpenter built it.
An old carpenter down on his luck,
flat out of bucks and with no contract,
a house as purely simple note
to whatever world walked by.

A Perspective: Lighthouse Reached by Dock

The eye arrows down the dock's platform
to the lighthouse, directing the mind
to the object it deems worth consideration,
herding all others into categories:
left, right;
lake, sky; wind
and the intrusion of motion,
not as important as the view's
invitation to examine. Concentrate,
the perspective implores, leave behind
the little house of your desire, where everything
inside must be made clear. Even now, something
is happening inside your head. Something decisive.
See? Something that needed to quit drumming is
    abandoned.

At Work

Dark spring morning.
Rain still upon us.

Dark face, glowering sockets,
the clock's. Old red eyes.

I shut them up with mine.

All night I was in an under room,
talking about poems.

The dead spoke some lines.
As if they'd return

for a certain sound.
I'm listening.

Heart! You'll not be hurt
when my shoulders fold about you.

I'll get up now,
and fix cabbage soup for today.

Let the rain pour down.

Another House

Here we are in another house,
unfinished, each room
sketched by joists. We go
from sorrow to sorrow,
sleeve-brushing encounters.

I won't have it.
I have it.
I'm angry.
I'm sorry.
Swing, swing.

You are steady,
low and steady.
You are fleeing,
leaving
no note behind.

Recognition

Of their love, I knew too much,
yet not enough.

They return in scanty scenes
at night, telling me everything

that is wordless, using gestures
to break down walls between us.

Don't they know I've forgiven them?
What more can I do?

They keep coming, sending
messages and warnings,

mirrors I'm supposed to
look into.

Reins

In the kitchen,
that small space
between porch door and oven,
my mother stood behind me
and braided my hair,
a sun-bleached mane in her hands.

Three strands she wove
over and under, a design
twisting the future
with the lost, her past,
until two long ropes
hung down my back.

On this dreamy morning,
long after her funeral,
my mother tugs, left
and right on my head,
in no hurry, she nor I,
to let go.

Phenomenon

Cats have known the trick forever:
a new chance lies behind every door.
I obey ours when they command:
Open this cupboard. Let me in.
They turn a shelf into a room, small,
safe, though never entirely safe, but
face-saving protection, a niche,
unlocked, an improvisation on space,
a variation on sliding behind a book.
Let's say we mentioned this ingenuity
in a woman's obituary:
She had a long life, years of making
a million rooms to hide in, out of almost
nothing but desperation and pure air.

III

To Live

Early in the morning something passed by.
It might have been human.
It left a trace under the trees:
on the path, a broken flower stem.

The day wore on, showing its stress.
The air melted in the heat.
The petals curled and shriveled.
The grass parched underfoot,

a tactic to go to sleep. Then I
came along, took the stem to my room,
put it in water; hours passed.
It greened, its bells turned lavender again.

This parable lies hidden everywhere.

The Accent on Flat

Flat, the land is flat.
Like our accent—our r's

growl as they circle their
nests in the uvular cave.

Our eyeballs flatten, staring
at this sheet of land. Even

the voice, exalted in the vault
above the tongue, in

imitation of heaven, even
the voice goes flat.

And I think of certain women
as worn-down mountains,

women who set their
hearts down to sing.

He Leadeth Me Beside the Still Waters

A voice promises water and grazing rights, in the end,
after westward expansion, an opening to land without
    end.

In the hills, Philistines, Indians, Turks, trogs, grass, oil,
silver, gold. A life strapped, swindled from start to end.

Wind howls overhead like fire. Among the boulders, wild
demands attack the backs of their prey, a furious end.

The shepherd's rod and staff turn into cudgels. This
valley will be lonely; loneliness can serve its own end.

Suddenly in the path, a table. Bread, I command. It
    appears.
I weep. Food in plenitude extends to the table's end.

How sweet the hand that presses a balm to my forehead!
How cool that hand! My hot, narrow misery ends.

On my left hand walks goodness; on my right, mercy.
I shall not want, my cup, my borders run over without end.

On the Ocean's Beach

Something cheery then. Something warm,
something to make love upon. Something
fun. Something to run into and get wet,
feel the tug of something stronger, much
surroundier than you are or ever will be.
No need to compete here. Ha! Something
to jump and be happy over in small measures,
content with duckling waddles, accepting
the little hour you can make or be and so
tickled pink about it you laugh. Something
that makes the bare feet feel at home again.
"This is the life!" they grin. Something
attracting birds and all manner of mollusks.
Something that's somewhere far away it some-
times seems. Some vision we come from,
that we celebrate vaguely on birthdays, that
salty caress rising sometimes in dreams.

Birch Trees

The birch stand in uneven rows of black and white,
their translation of soft rain falling.

Their vertical script, older than the fifth century,
younger than the birth of the Mississippi,

precursor to haiku and tanka, their shadows stressed
by the brush of a crow's wing. They've mastered

image and impression. Their genius is to capture
silence and space, from left to right, up or down.

What seems backwards among them moves forwards.
No language is sure how or why this moves.

Moon

It rises from the ocean as it does on a sea of prairie.
One moon in a thousand places.

Moonlight dyes the water red,
veils wheat fields in rose.

Who can go to bed tonight
with a whole heart?

Six Days After

35W Bridge collapse, August 1, 2007

I want to tell you a simple story.
This morning, in the evergreen,
under the sprinkler's spray,
a goldfinch took a shower
every ten seconds. And if delight
is hopping from branch to wet
branch, her time in the tree was
all outbursts of bliss.
The tree sparkled, too.
The bird flew away;
two droplets stayed glistening
for about ten minutes,
then they disappeared.
This happened on a day
not as muggy as August first,
in a yard not far from the river,
and seen by a woman who used
the bridge that collapsed but didn't
drive over it the day it fell. And now
she watches with renewed fascination
scenes in her back yard and collects
whatever joy she can when it is present.

Last Syllables

In the last hour, the water is cold
as crank handles in winter,
and the river can't feel
the weight of a hand, as if any
were strong enough to cup
the river's power. The waves
lap, panicky, witless
against the changing shore.
Currents move like muscles
struggling; no one beside the bed
can understand their swirls.
Detached company, people
are more distant than ever,
though the river still deciphers
voices from debris, waving
in morphine on a silty bottom.
What is clear draws the river's
mouth into its final, astonished gape.
The ocean it is becoming.

Sparse Music

For the marriage
of moon to clouds,
wind came with a broken arm.

Clouds were high and thin,
two-fingered. Sky hid its face
behind their cold doubts.

For the ceremony
the grass wore brown and dun,
a costume more like an end.

Snow had yet to arrive,
had not covered the ground
with its feathery train.

Orpheus's Shadow

In mountains where Orpheus was born
       I fell in love
            with the kingdom of Thrace.

I, the hunchback,
         who overheard the King's secret
         and never revealed it.

Blame it on me, the loss to the world.
      Let history denounce me daily.
         What you've never experienced

you can't miss. I'm the one
     whose days are long
         haunted by my freedom.

Gourds

Unlikely
candidates for imitation—
off by themselves in the garden,
rattling their odd colors,
turtle shell green,
dried bone, dust orange,
tooth yellow,
the fathering bee long ago flown away.

Someone connected,
copied their shape,
hollowed out a wooden heart,
strung strings
for the mandolinist to strum
over the void.

Lilacs

A bouquet of lilacs, big as a bush,
lush, rich, a translation from Tristan
and Isolde's purple song of tumescence.
In my room, present as inheritance,
a fragrance in remembrance of flesh.
Only the sidewalks' neighborliness
restrains the lilacs' opulence, their
relentless busty business, the noise
they make in the street, their genius
favored by gods of scent and color.
Even in an old bush brittleness breaks out
of its gooseneck pattern to become a stroke
we love to feel on our lips and throat and thighs.

Headstones

They have to last. That's why
granite is the likely choice
for their composition. They have
to stand up to the Northern Plains,
its fierce summers, its scouring
winter wind and the earth
sinking under their foundations.
They have to be dutiful, loyal to
the name and dates inscribed
on their chests, good soldiers
though constant failures, unable
to convey any further correspondence.

Navigation by Metaphor

So what is this? An animal
split wide open to reveal
the blue gut that functions within?

If you're lucky, your god has wings
and a house for a head you can crawl
into for comfort. Woods, too.

Not enough trees to be a forest,
but having a river, a blue canal,
coursing from north to night.

The sky will offer derision.
Why are you marrying this? it'll ask.
Are there no clouds left for you to choose?

Cow, a Pastoral

She's wandered loose from pasture,
now she must rest. She's parked
her arse beside a country lane,
to study her shadow, doze in the sun
on a lovely, expansive late afternoon.
There's grass to munch, that which she lies in.
An old cow, wise beyond her rump.
She ignores her teats, aching to be milked.
Before nightfall the farmer will come,
geehawing her name with a git-on-home.
Her resumé, her udder.
She, who loved milk as a calf, is fated
to pass its peace on to the world.

The Animals

unsigned painting, 17th century style

They'll inhabit an ark which is, here, a long house,
shaped like a slipper, with a barn door in its side.
A seaworthy vessel, if you've never seen a sea.
Its only criterion is balsam's: to stay afloat
on God's darkest breath. The animals are
a patient lot. Sheep graze not far from the lion.
Tigers rollick but not enough to frighten llamas
or giraffes.   A pair of black and white steeds,
delicate as dancers, lead the oxen to the plank.

They're the great noise they would have made
had the waters rolled over them. The painter's mind,
a moving territory, seems pleased that elephants,
big rump rhinos, and its own half moose-half bear
can be saved. Look. Through a pale green fog
you can make out, on the far shore, Sodom & Gomorrah.
Rain's starting; animals, boarding. The lion's human
face is an aside to the audience. Is this boondoggle
or apocalypse? Sooty clouds warn of the fire to come.

In Ascent

My name is bird.
Here is my creed:
to fly, to glide, to hover,
to dip and wheel, to soar.
I change in light,
my color born of snow.
I move by light.
The evening stills me.
Here is my comfort:
my strength, my weakness,
my cry, my song.
I can't tell where
it begins or ends—
in the rabbit's gut,
in a cloud's moods,
in my wings at night.
I ascend and descend.
I light. I live.

New Water

for Archie and Sharon

All those years—almost a hundred—
the farm had hard water.
Hard orange. Buckets lined in orange.
Sink and tub and toilet, too,
once they got running water.
And now, in less than a lifetime,
just by changing the well's location,
in the same yard, mind you,
the water's soft, clear, delicious to drink.
All those years to shake your head over.
Look how sweet life has become;
you can see it in the couple who live here,
their calmness as they sit at their table,
the beauty as they offer you new water to drink.

IV

Life Is Such a Great Beast

Who are these people I pass in the street?
What are they like? What lurks inside
their bodies? Old age, accidents, regrets,
twitches of happiness? Who knows when
their stories' X will happen? Which night
will become for them an eternity?
Shouldn't this slow the crowd down?
Make every swallow even more
sensual in a young woman's throat?
I'm passing emperors, empresses
of the daily whose hour builds
and fades with every step they make.
Sometimes I whisper *God bless you*
because I don't know any other concept
large enough to cover so many people.

The Kiss

for Alfonso Wu
Chinese Old Folks Home, Havana

He wants to know my name.
He leans closer to watch my lips
repeat it.   He wants the last name, too.
Ah, that one has to be chopped up,
fed to him in small bites, still,
too much for his tongue; his lips
mime mine; we're nose to nose.
He wants to know what's wrong.
Why the canes? I slide my hands
over my hips, *la problema.*
Ah! his lips contort,
he knows how it will be for me
when I'm his age, so old
I can't remember when I was born.
Ah! he woos, so close I fall
in love with his breath, the sweet
quivering of it, ah, now he wants to
name me, softly, in my ear.
"Pobrecita." Poor you.

Zippers

I had a seamstress friend who spent two years in Hamburg
doing buttonholes. Once the buttonhole was conquered,
—my kingdom for a buttonhole—she moved on to design,
looking down her nose at zippers, their tiny levers
and steel tracks. Such is the demand of art, an arachnidan
stitch, leaving a silken trace across cloth.

You need a northwest wind to test buttons vs. zippers,
the Palisades' breezes won't do, a bigger blast is called for,
a wind in which your appearance means nothing. Let two
men stand on a butte near the Missouri. Whose coat keeps
    warm
as a rabbit in its burrow under snow? Whose lets in a chill,
eventually pops, frigidly revealing the solitary chest alone?

Guards in the Pushkin Museum

No one will take begging lessons from the gypsies.
Especially not the old women who need them,
who, in a rickety hour, took their money
from the mattress and handed it to a Russian banker,
a mistake they'll work the rest of their lives for,

one to a room, back to the wall, avoiding your eyes,
stopping you from touching crumbling objects.
If they laid on you a most genteel panhandle—
Please, I have no money, no savings, no pension, no hus-
        band,
I lost him at Stalingrad—you'd see in their palms

a reminder of Lenin, the sickle-shaped heart line.
A deep cut around the thumb. Not to be re-opened.
They keep their hands tucked under sweatered elbows,
guarding their borders. They go on, standing like willows
while every ruble you have on you weighs a ton.

Telegram

Here it comes, out of the universe,
over ocean, mountains, high plains,
following a river from its headwaters,
down a gravel road to the front door, 306,
a house as yet without telephone.

There she is, sitting on the edge
of the made bed; it's late morning,
beds are made by eight. Telegram,
balled-up beside her. In her lap, a photo,
a marine in uniform. He's smiling,

white-toothed. She's weeping, blue.
The telegram looks weak now,
but the effect, in total, is soul, breaking.
The noise it makes! Little
clutches of breath that won't stop.

For the Woman Who Gave Her Last Coin

Today is the day the psalmist made,
made of the dark a city in sapphire,
barred the gate with rubies and joy,
studded the steps Ma ascends into stars,

stepping over the ordinary miracle of death.
Oh, palace! Oh, banquet! Ma feels enough
at home to fill water glasses for the men.
See what she could have left behind!

Today is the day the psalmist promised.
Even the rich are thrown scraps from plates.
And the woman who gave her last coin marches
beside the Wizard into the Hall of Love.

Story of a Farm Girl

Here's how she wound up in Minneapolis:
Out on the prairie the grandparents' grain
flowed from the wagon bed into the elevator.
Money was exchanged. The elevator operator
shipped the grain to the mill city on the Great Northern.
More money was exchanged. Money made
busy streets, buildings, offices for workers
like the farm girl, trading her earnestness
for bread and room. Years passed like this;
on the girl's weekends she discovered the arts.
So did elevators. The prairie Byzantium
some people named them. Spare and surreal
as towers in a Spanish western, the vertical
stacked against the railroad's horizontal,
leading to the edge of the horizon and beyond.
Long ago she'd played a game like that,
lining up kitchen chairs across waves of blue
linoleum, riding imagination into the unknown.

The Queen: On the Occasion of the King's Burial

After the crowd's wail and crush,
after the Beloved's body
is carried off in its coffin by the men,
and the white-scarved women
at windows follow its journey
through the streets with mourning eyes,

after the sons and dignitaries
file from the cemetery, the Queen
may enter, quite alone, like the woman
who stole very early to the tomb.
She acquaints herself with her husband's
new bed, its four, separate corners.

Hush now, he sleeps. The queen
lets no little outbreaks of grief run loose.

Goosegirl

fairy tale, brought up to date

These eternal three tasks!
And then three more.
And then the prince.
And then the marriage.
And then the chores and the occasional
fleeting thought, while feeding the geese,
to be rid of them all.
And the rush of warmth
from the heat of this thought.

More duty. More afternoons
spent in the stable
of maddening reasoning.
And then the wild
abandonment of decision:

Changing the house lock,
bolting the shutters,
refusing to answer the door.

Anyone who fumbles
with the old key,
never let in.

Not the door pounders.
Not the criers
in the rainswept road.

Let us in! Let us in! It's raining.
You've got all of our clothes in there.

This is ridiculous! We've had no supper!
Our spare cash is lying in the drawer!

Do you want us to sleep out here?
Do you want us to freeze out here?
Do you want us to die out here?
Do you really want us to go away?

Goosegirl! Goosegirl!
Let us in, and we'll make you queen!

Bar Scene

A mouse is a giant
to a cockroach
or an ant. A mouse
with its red eyes
glowing in the dark
is hell's own fire. A mouse
with a cigarette is
someone you can't tell,
Hey, no smoking here,
no drinking. What
does a martini do
to a little stomach?
Think of the mountains
of anger at cats
released, sideways
at anyone, anything, nearby!
That's why the blind
cockroach senses
it must stay away
from a mouse paw.
That's why an ant
shoulders its crumb
quickly into a hole.
That's why a memory
can be so fearful.

The Gus I Knew

There wasn't one grass blade higher than another
in his yard. Not one fleck of red paint peeling
on the barn or any other shed; the white trim,
bright. And when one morning, early,
he went out into the barn, and made an end
with his gun, he fell on straw where any
blood puddle could easily be hefted
with a pitchfork and carried out.

In Sickness and in Health

I watched them holding hands, two old lovers.
I watched how she clung to his. I kept watching.
I saw how he, after a while, slipped out of her grasp;
I guessed her hand was too warm for him.
Or, he'd forgotten who she was and found
hand-holding with a stranger awkward.
Or, he'd regressed to his own solitude
and wanted his hands free to wander
or wonder at the vast openness he held,
leaving her beside him to feel the separation
alone, her hand's emptiness, that confusion.

So Many Kinds of Theatre

Have you heard the story of New Zealanders,
trying to save a beached whale and her calf?
The humans were at the point of giving up,
the whale, too, when a dolphin came swimming along

and talked to the whale, talked in a language
humans don't understand, and the whale
rolled and followed the dolphin, the whale and her calf
slipped into the bay, swam into the ocean,

never to be seen again. True story. At the end,
the New Zealanders stood cheering. Rows of them,
on the beach.
                        Why wouldn't we humans
invent theatre? Why wouldn't we want to see
plays where the defeated triumph and go on?

The Widow's Door

That night the voices she'd thought were outside
her bedroom window came from inside, her living room.
    Oh!
Her thoughts matched, utterly, her struggling heart

and frantic whispers to 911. Like a shadow,
staying close to the hallway wall, she used the dark
as tunnel, buffer, trickster with a bag of blinding

powder. It showed her how to move, cunning,
silent, oh, always so silent, quiet, stealthy,
gaining on the back door exit.
                              Once reached,

police flooded in, guns drawn. Lights clicked on,
boot steps clumped through the rooms, waking
two drunks on the carpet. Hand cuffs snapped on.

The bleary-eyed, led away. Later, after police
had searched the house, assuring her no one else
lurked in a closet, what she returned to was

her heart in darkness, and how it flew,
circling, fluttering, plummeting,
when she realized she was no longer alone.

The Story of Diana and Actaeon

"Diana and Actaeon"
Jacob Jordaens, c. 1640

Actaeon comes upon them, Diana and her friends,
lounging naked after a night hunt, their skin, moon-pale.

The scent of sex stops him in his tracks, he stands still
as a dog points, smelling fox in a field.

One will triumph over the other. For a man
a fox, a deer are easy to hunt down with his hounds.

(So unlike the sun's and moon's ephemeral,
rainbow-tinted dogs, circling the cold eye's range.)

He wants to bag Diana, too, her happiness.
But that great hunt has never endured

uninvited interruptions. The moon's dark side.
One look from her and Actaeon's pierced, his dogs

sink their teeth into his heart. Tonight the great
huntress shines over a stag's pool of dark blood.

Juggling

"The Juggler"
Marc Chagall, 1943

If I could really see,
as sometimes I'm led to,

the man dancing down the street
is really juggling

his love affair
with the things of this world

encircling him. In love,
he has grown huge, heavy

wings for he must also be
part bird; how can you dance

without flying, without taking
great leaps? All the while

his love, dressed in a pretty,
sky-blue gown with a long, lacy train,

waits for him in the wings,
her heart beating fast.

Everything

At the corner of Cain's and Molstead's,
I turn west toward the river, following the tracks

to the viaduct, where the smell of creosote
seeps from the pillars and dirt bolstering it.

I skip from railroad tie to tie, my legs, surly.
I imagine a diesel coming, the pounding rails;

me, the coin, squashed flat. In the whistle's
blast, my mother's, "Stay away from the tracks!"

I take the rest of my life left and leap
backwards, off the rails; now they lie

shimmering in summer heat and silence.
Grasshoppers fly at my jeans, snapping, loud

enough to be a good scare. But they are not
rattlers. I wade through weeds and blown paper

to a dirt road, a valley of ruts and grooves,
to Schlecht's, a house with encampment,

ramshackle as a stable with wing-additions.
A scrub tub squats on the open stoop.

And there stands Mrs. Schlecht, shaped like the rain
barrel, her face white with heat, her hair limp.

In her kitchen I drink syrup from canned pineapple,
then head back home, having tasted the world.